SURPRISINGLY SCARY!

Look Out for the BLUE-RINGED OCTOPUS!

Alana Olsen

PowerKiDS press.
New York

Published in 2016 by The Rosen Publishing Group, Inc.
29 East 21st Street, New York, NY 10010

First Edition

Editor: Caitlin McAneney
Book Design: Katelyn Heinle

Photo Credits: Cover Richard Merritt FRPS/Moment/Getty Images; back cover, pp. 2–24 (background) CAMPINCOOL/Shutterstock.com; p. 5 aquapix/Shutterstock.com; p. 7 (main) dive-hive/Shutterstock.com; p. 7 (map) ekler/Shutterstock.com; p. 9 Believe.../Moment/Getty Images; p. 11 Chris Newbert/Minden Pictures/Getty Images; p. 13 (main) YUSRAN ABDUL RAHMAN/Shutterstock.com; p. 13 (inset) Gary Ombler/Dorling Kindersley/Getty Images; p. 15 (main) kaschibo/Shutterstock.com; p. 15 (inset) Rich Carey/Shutterstock.com; p. 17 Chris Fertnig/E+/Getty Images; p. 19 scubaluna/Shutterstock.com; p. 21 Chanwit Whanset/Shutterstock.com; p. 22 © iStockphoto.com/dsi.

Library of Congress Cataloging-in-Publication Data

Olsen, Alana, author.
Look out for the blue-ringed octopus! / Alana Olsen.
pages cm. — (Surprisingly scary!)
Includes bibliographical references and index.
ISBN 978-1-4994-0877-5 (pbk.)
ISBN 978-1-4994-0893-5 (6 pack)
ISBN 978-1-4994-0934-5 (library binding)
1. Blue-ringed octopuses—Juvenile literature. 2. Dangerous aquatic animals—Juvenile literature. I. Title.
QL430.3.O2O47 2015
594.56—dc23

2014050042

Manufactured in the United States of America

CPSIA Compliance Information: Batch #WS15PK: For Further Information contact Rosen Publishing, New York, New York at 1-800-237-9932

CONTENTS

Stay Away! 4
Finding the Blue-Ringed Octopus 6
Way to Glow! 8
Sneak Attack! 10
A Bite That Kills 12
No Easy Prey 14
Watch Out! 16
How to Stay Safe 18
Helping the Octopus 20
Friends from Far Away 22
Glossary 23
Index 24
Websites 24

STAY AWAY!

Imagine you're visiting a **coral reef** and you see something glowing. It's a small octopus with bright blue circles all over its body. Stay away—it's a blue-ringed octopus!

The blue-ringed octopus is a small but deadly ocean creature. Its glowing skin makes it a cool creature to find. Some people try to collect them or buy them to put in tanks at home. However, this isn't safe, because the blue-ringed octopus has strong **venom** in each bite.

Blue-ringed octopuses hide along the floor of shallow waters. They aren't found in deep water.

SURPRISINGLY TRUE!

There are a few species, or kinds, of blue-ringed octopuses. Some have bigger rings than others.

FINDING THE BLUE-RINGED OCTOPUS

Where can you find blue-ringed octopuses? These tiny octopuses can be found in waters from Australia to Japan. This is sometimes called the Indo-Pacific **region** because it includes areas in both the Indian and the Pacific Oceans. This area includes island countries, such as Papua New Guinea, Indonesia, and the Solomon Islands.

Blue-ringed octopuses live around coral reefs and in tide pools. Tide pools are pools on the seashore that hold many creatures. Ocean water flows into the pools when the tide is high.

Blue-ringed octopuses like to hide in sandy areas. They also like to hide between rocks.

SURPRISINGLY TRUE!

Blue-ringed octopuses are so small they can hide in seashells and soda cans on the ocean floor.

WAY TO GLOW!

You can tell a blue-ringed octopus by its features. The soft body of a blue-ringed octopus is only about the size of a golf ball. It has eight arms covered in suckers that help the octopus grab things. With its arms stretched out, the octopus is about eight inches (20 cm) long.

The octopus's body is normally tan, yellow, or gray. It's covered in blue rings with brown centers. It has a hard beak under its body to bite and chew things.

A blue-ringed octopus's rings are usually faded and hard to see, but they start to glow bright blue when the octopus is scared.

SURPRISINGLY TRUE!

The blue-ringed octopus has special color-filled pouches and glowing **layers** of skin under its top layer of skin. It squeezes these to turn its rings bright blue.

Blue-ringed octopuses may even be able to spray their venom into the water to **paralyze** their prey before they attack.

SURPRISINGLY TRUE!

Unlike other kinds of octopuses, most adult blue-ringed octopuses don't have an ink sac. This means they can't spray ink into the water to help them hide.

A BITE THAT KILLS

A blue-ringed octopus's venom is very strong. In fact, it's stronger than the venom of any land animal and any other octopus. Its venom doesn't just kill crabs. The venom from one bite is enough to kill 26 people!

The octopus's venom is made in two **glands** inside its body. One gland makes venom to kill prey, and the other gland makes venom to fight predators. The venom mixes with the octopus's saliva, or spit. It's usually forced into a person or animal through a bite.

A blue-ringed octopus bites with its beak. An octopus's beak looks a lot like the beak of a bird.

SURPRISINGLY TRUE!

Each venom gland in a blue-ringed octopus is often as large as its brain.

NO EASY PREY

With such strong venom, it may seem like the blue-ringed octopus is the top predator in its **environment**. However, this octopus is very small. Larger fish, such as the moray eel and sharks, often eat blue-ringed octopuses.

The blue-ringed octopus has certain **defenses** it uses to keep safe. The octopus uses camouflage, or makes itself the same color as its surroundings. It can turn tan or yellow like the sand so predators can't see it. It can flatten itself or curl up in a hole to hide.

A blue-ringed octopus's rings don't glow when it's hiding. That makes it harder to see. However, when a predator spots the octopus, the rings will glow bright blue. That warns the predator that the octopus is venomous and will bite!

MORAY EEL

SURPRISINGLY TRUE!

The moray eel and the blue-ringed octopus can fight to the death. The eel is much bigger, but the octopus is very venomous.

WATCH OUT!

Luckily for humans, blue-ringed octopuses don't want to eat us. They're shy and want us to leave them alone.

However, sometimes people step on blue-ringed octopuses when they're walking in water. Some people pick them up, not knowing they'll bite. When a blue-ringed octopus bites, a person is in big trouble. The bite might not hurt too much, but within seconds or minutes, the person will lose their senses of sight and touch. They won't be able to speak or swallow.

In minutes, a person bitten by a blue-ringed octopus will become paralyzed. Their lungs will stop working so they can't breathe.

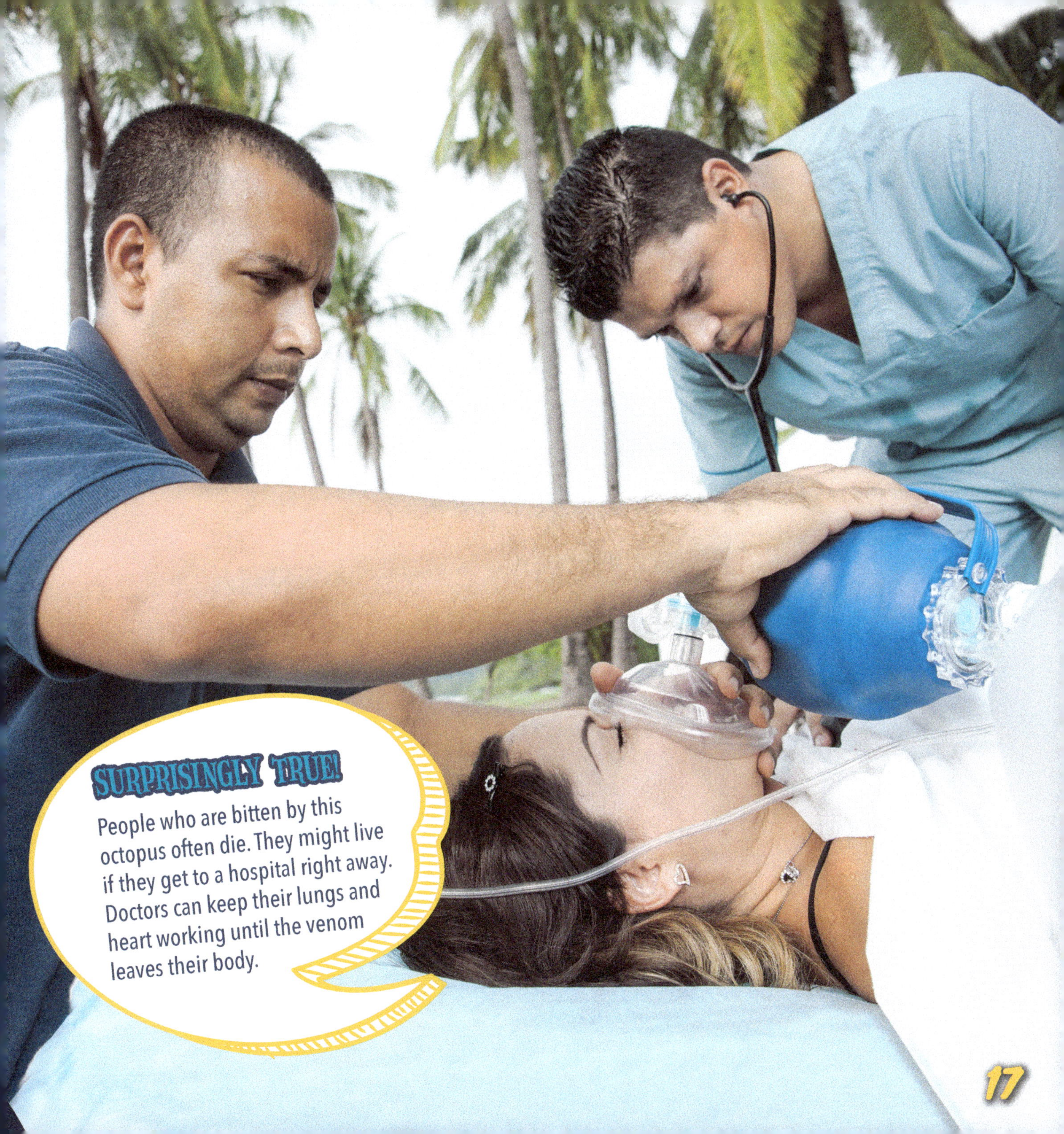

SURPRISINGLY TRUE!

People who are bitten by this octopus often die. They might live if they get to a hospital right away. Doctors can keep their lungs and heart working until the venom leaves their body.

HOW TO STAY SAFE

Bites from blue-ringed octopuses kill people. That's why it's important to know how to keep yourself safe from this ocean animal.

First, never pick up a blue-ringed octopus. Never try to bring it home to keep as a pet. If you live near beaches with these octopuses, be careful while walking in the water. Shuffle your feet so the octopus will know you're there and swim away. Last, never buy this animal as a pet. Some people keep them in tanks, but this isn't safe for the octopus or the owner.

People who keep these octopuses as pets can harm both the octopus and other people. Other people might not know it's venomous and might try to touch it.

SURPRISINGLY TRUE!

People with big saltwater tanks sometimes keep small octopuses, such as the California two-spot octopus. It's not as venomous as its blue-ringed cousin!

HELPING THE OCTOPUS

This octopus is not endangered, or at risk of dying out. However, it's our duty to make sure this glowing octopus lives for many years to come.

The greatest risk to the blue-ringed octopus is people **invading** its environment. Its environment might be ruined when people build near the water or dump waste in it. People might trap the octopus to keep or sell as a pet. These animals are becoming popular pets because they don't ink in tanks.

Octopuses are usually caught with nets, hands, fishing lines, or pots.

SURPRISINGLY TRUE!

There are no laws to help keep the blue-ringed octopus safe. Because of that, people sometimes treat it without care.

that's a sign that this cool creature is definitely deadly and wants you to stay far away!

GLOSSARY

coral reef: The hard remains of coral animals that form a line in warm, shallow ocean waters.

defense: A feature of a living thing that helps keep it safe.

environment: Everything that surrounds a living thing.

gland: A body part that produces something that helps with a bodily function.

invade: To enter into a place and cause harm.

layer: One thickness lying over or under another.

paralyze: To make something unable to move.

prey: An animal hunted by other animals for food.

region: A large space of land that has things in common.

venom: A type of poison made by an animal and passed to another animal by a sting or bite.

INDEX

A

arms, 8, 10

B

beak, 8, 12, 13, 22

bite, 4, 8, 12, 14, 16, 18

body, 4, 8, 12, 17

C

camouflage, 14

coral reef, 4, 6

D

defenses, 14

G

glands, 12, 13

glowing, 4, 8, 9, 14, 20, 22

I

Indian Ocean, 6, 7

P

Pacific Ocean, 6, 7

people, 4, 12, 16, 17, 18, 20, 21, 22

pet, 18, 20

predators, 10, 12, 14

prey, 10, 12, 14

R

rings, 5, 8, 9, 14, 22

S

skin, 4, 9

sneak attack, 10, 22

T

tanks, 4, 18, 19, 20

tide pools, 6

V

venom, 4, 10, 12, 13, 14, 15, 17, 18, 20, 22

WEBSITES

Due to the changing nature of Internet links, PowerKids Press has developed an online list of websites related to the subject of this book. This site is updated regularly. Please use this link to access the list: www.powerkidslinks.com/surp/oct